Applesauce Grows on Trees

Anna & family
Love,
Aunt Phyllis

Written by Phyllis Barrett Samara, OTR/L
and Jennifer MacNeil

Illustrated by Sarah Ruth Forde

Cover Design by Meg Nicole MacNeil

Dedicated to my loving mother and role model, Amalia Raspe Barrett, and to the shared love we have for all children and their families—P.B.S.

A special thank you to my professional mentors A. Jean Ayers, Ph.D., OTR, Lucy Jane Miller, Ph.D., OTR/L and Kay A. Toomey, Ph.D. to whom I credit the foundation of my sensory integration and feeding approach. —P.B.S.

Printed in the United States of America
First Printing, 2014
Printed by CreateSpace, an Amazon.com Company
ISBN-13: 978-1502865786
ISBN-10: 1502865785

Ordering Information:
Available for purchase through www.amazon.com and other retail outlets. Special discounts are available on quantity purchases by corporations, associations, bookstores and wholesalers. For details, contact Barrett Family Wellness Center, Inc. at the address below.

Attention Barrett Sensory Book Series
Barrett Family Wellness Center, Inc.
107 Otis Street
Northborough, MA 01532
508-898-2688
books@barrettfamilywellness.com
www.BarrettFamilyWellness.com/index.php/barrett-sensory-book-series

My name is Sam. If you ask me, all food should be white.

Bread, cheese and applesauce are my favorite. I eat them every day. They taste good to me and they fill me up.

I don't understand why my family wants me to eat other stuff. Something about this word "nutrition." It's supposed to help my body grow and be strong.

Today, my mom and dad are bringing me to meet Ms. Phyllis. She is a person who loves food. All food: white, green, red, orange and brown things too.

I am a little worried about meeting her because I don't know what to expect. I don't think I want her to ask me to eat something new.

I like bread, cheese and applesauce. They are perfect for me.

Ms. Phyllis came out to the waiting room to get us. She was happy and friendly and asked if I was ready to play.

Play?

I thought we were going to talk about that word "nutrition" and colorful foods.

I like to play.

Ms. Phyllis asked if I wanted to ride a big wheel to the Snack Shack. I was excited by that. Riding a big wheel down the hallway was fun!

I rode past rooms filled with colorful toys, swings and ramps. There were lots of other children there too. They were playing with all sorts of things.

I liked this place!

I parked the big wheel outside the door with the "Snack Shack" sign.

"Want to play catch?" Ms. Phyllis asked me.

"Ok," I said.

She tossed me a red apple from the bowl on the table. I was surprised. I didn't want anyone to ask me to eat the apple, but holding it like a ball was ok. I tossed it back to her.

"Now, let's roll the apple across the table!" exclaimed Ms. Phyllis.

Back and forth we rolled the red apple. The apple felt smooth and firm. It was ok to touch. Ms. Phyllis was doing all sorts of crazy spins with the apple. The apple was zigging and zagging all over the table. It made me laugh.

Mom and Dad played too. I have never seen them roll apples before.
I laughed harder.

"I know!" exclaimed Ms. Phyllis. "Let's make an apple car!"

Ms. Phyllis cut one big, fat slice out of the apple for each of us.

"Hold these for me while we get some more parts for the car," said Ms. Phyllis.

The apple felt different now. It was slippery and wet on the white inside and smooth on the outside part.

Ms. Phyllis opened the cabinets and asked me to pick out something round that we could use for wheels. I chose a colorful box of round cereal.

"Now, can you pick a round food from the fridge too?" asked Ms. Phyllis.

"How about the green grapes?" I asked.

"Fantastic choice," said Ms. Phyllis.

"Oh, smell that yummy smell!" suggested Ms. Phyllis. "So sweet!"

I put my nose sort of close to the apple and gave it a little whiff.

"It does smell sort of sweet," I said. "But I don't like apples."

Ms. Phyllis handed me two toothpicks to use as wheel axles. The apple made a crunchy noise when the toothpick went through.

We opened the cereal box and poured out a small pile of Fruit O's. I picked up a purple cereal circle and slid it on a toothpick, but it fell off. My mom tried an orange circle. Her cereal fell off too.

"Guess the cereal center is too big for our toothpick axles," said Ms. Phyllis. "Let's try the grapes."

My dad sliced eight grapes in half and handed us all four pieces each.

The grapes felt more slippery than the apples. The grapes were easy to stick onto the toothpicks, and they stayed on.

Just before I put my last grape half on the toothpick, Ms. Phyllis asked if I might be ready to smell the grape. I thought smelling it would be ok. Playing with it hadn't been too hard.

"Is the grape sweeter smelling than the apple?" Ms. Phyllis asked me.

I smelled the grape, then the apple. I wasn't sure. I smelled both again.

"I just don't know," I answered.

"If you are ready to take a little lick, perhaps your tongue could help you make a decision," suggested Ms. Phyllis.

I leaned in closer to the grape and gave it a teeny, tiny lick. I looked at the apple, carefully moved it to just touching my lip and gave it an itsy, bitsy lick too.

"I just don't know which one is sweeter," I said.

"How about you pretend to brush your teeth with each one?" suggested Ms. Phyllis. "Try to brush as many times as you are old."

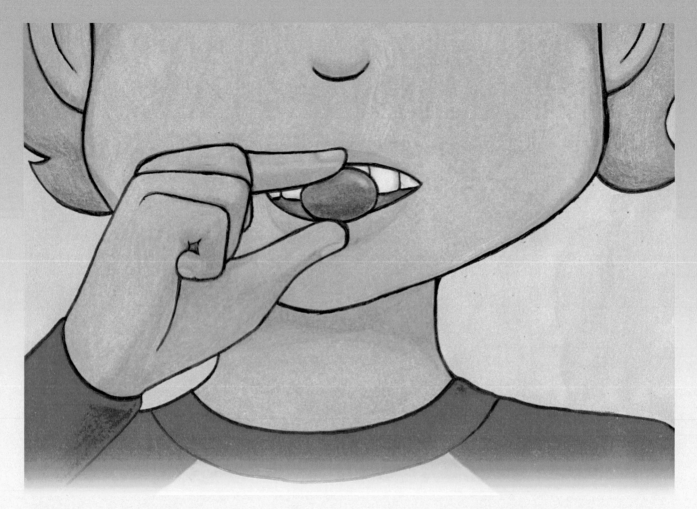

I held the apple like a toothbrush as best as I could and brushed up and down six times. It felt weird. The apple left sweet juicy spots on my teeth.

I pinched the grape between my fingers. One...Two... It fell out of my mouth.

"Don't worry about that," said Ms. Phyllis. "What do you think?"

"I think my apple is sweeter," I said.

Ms. Phyllis got an excited look on her face.

"Let's make applesauce!" she exclaimed.

I had never made applesauce. I never thought about where applesauce came from. I thought it came from a jar.

Wait! Apples grow on trees. Does that mean applesauce grows on trees?

Ms. Phyllis peeled the apple in long, thin peels. She asked me if I could throw away the skins for her. I could do that! When I picked them up, they wrapped around my wrists like bracelets. They felt cold and wet.

I opened the trash lid with the foot pedal and shook the peels off my wrists. They stuck to the edges of the trash can when I threw them in. My hands felt sticky. I washed them off in the sink. They felt better to me now.

Ms. Phyllis cut the apples into little chunks and placed them in a glass bowl with some water. We put them in the microwave and set the time to cook for two minutes.*

"MMMmm…Doesn't that smell yummy?" asked Ms. Phyllis. "Warm apples have a stronger smell to me than raw apples just sitting on the counter."

When the microwave beeped, Ms. Phyllis placed the bowl of warmed apple chunks back on the table. She handed me a spoon and asked if I could mash them.

*Recipe on page 24

Before my eyes, one of my favorite foods began to appear. Applesauce! I love applesauce! I couldn't believe we had just made it. I looked over at the bowl of apples. I looked back at my dish of applesauce.

"Mom, can we make this at home?" I asked.

"Of course we can," answered Mom.

"Are you ready to take a taste, Chef Sam?" asked Ms. Phyllis.

My stomach went funny. She was asking me to eat something. I knew it!

But wait. I love applesauce. I made this applesauce. I was going to try it!

I lifted a spoonful of the warm applesauce close to my mouth.

"Blow on it. It's hot," said Ms. Phyllis.

I took a big breath in. I blew all over my spoon. I could see the steamy hot air blow off of the spoon. I was ready for a taste.

I put a little teeny tiny bit on my lip. I took an itsy bitsy lick of it with my tongue.

"It tastes like regular applesauce!" I exclaimed.

Only it was better. It was the best applesauce because I made it.

I was very proud.

"Mom and Dad, would you like to try my applesauce?" I asked.

"Absolutely," said Dad.

"You'd bet I do," said Mom.

"Don't forget to blow on it. It's hot," I reminded.

Mom and Dad both blew on their spoons and the steamy heat disappeared.

"Yum!" they both exclaimed.

My body felt happy and proud.

"How about we play again next week?" Ms. Phyllis suggested. " I am thinking about making mashed potato snowmen!"

I couldn't wait to see how she was going to have us do that.

Note to Parents/Educators

As a pediatric occupational and feeding therapist who believes strongly in sensory integration, I approach all my clients from a playful, non-stress evoking and sensory-filled angle. For problem eaters, I also base my therapeutic practice on "The SOS Approach to Feeding" developed by Kay A. Toomey, Ph.D. I let the child have a large part in the decision-making and experience so that their interest and curiosity grows.

In this story, I worked with a child who would not eat new or colorful foods. My first goal was to get Sam to touch a red food and then a green food. If we got that far, my second step was to have the child smell it. The third target was for Sam to taste it. Unlike this book, sometimes these objectives take weeks or even months. Trust needs to be built without being threatening in any way. My role is that of a "suggestor," not someone who will force someone to do anything. I am constantly thinking up new ways to reach children, and all children are different.

I also find it very important to connect what the child is eating to real food, not something packaged or canned. An understanding of eating healthy things is such an important foundation for us all as eaters. It takes just as much work to introduce junk food as it does healthy options.

You can do this too. I challenge you to make a fun process out of feeding your child(ren) something new today.

If you are struggling for ideas, please feel free to reach out to me. I can be contacted at books@barrettfamilywellness.com.

Phyllis B. Samara, OTR/L

Ms. Phyllis' Single Serving Applesauce Recipe

Mix the following ingredients in a microwavable bowl and heat for 2 minutes on high. Mash with spoon after it is heated. *A nice option is to add a dash of cinnamon.*

- One medium sized Macintosh apple, cut roughly into 1/2 inch cubes

- 1/4 cup of water

Bowl will be HOT!
I suggest an adult handle it for children.